Katie Greenall

FATTY FAT FAT

Salamander Street

PLAYS

First published in 2020 by Salamander Street Ltd.
(info@salamanderstreet.com)

Copyright © Katie Greenall, 2020

PB: 9781913630744
E: 9781913630737

Printed and bound in Great Britain

10 9 8 7 6 5 4 3 2 1

Katie Greenall

FATTY FAT FAT

Salamander Street

PLAYS

First published in 2020 by Salamander Street Ltd.
(info@salamanderstreet.com)

PB: 9781913630744
E: 9781913630737

Printed and bound in Great Britain

10 9 8 7 6 5 4 3 2 1

FATTY FAT FAT was developed with support from The Yard Theatre, Nuffield Southampton, Roundhouse and Arts Council England.

FATTY FAT FAT (FFF) debuted at VAULT Festival in 2019 where it won the VAULTS Origins Award for Outstanding New Work. FFF has been performed over 50 times across the UK, including a sold-out 5* run at Edinburgh Fringe Festival.

Creative Team:

Writer & Performer	Katie Greenall (She/They)
Producer	Daisy Hale (They/Them)
Director	Madelaine Moore (She/Her)
Lighting Designer	Lauren Woodhead (She/Her)
Sound Designer	Anna Clock (They/Them)
Movement Director	Rubyyy Jones (They/Them)
Dramaturg	Bridget Minamore (She/Her)
Assistant Producer	Sean Brooks (He/Him)
Stage Manager	Stacey Sandford (She/Her)
Artwork	Liberty Antonia Sadler (She/They)
Photo	Polly Bycroft- Brown (She/Her)

As part of an ongoing commitment to using *FATTY FAT FAT* as a platform for Fat Activism, engaging fat people in the show and creating fat communities across the UK, we employed ten Fat Folk from across England and Wales to make a team of *FATTY FAT FAT* Ambassadors.

We came together for the FAT SUMMIT on 29th February 2020 at the Southbank Centre London, where we planned our collective and individual activisms. This work is ongoing and consistently evolving, manifesting in many different ways from zines to local fat Facebook groups.

FATTY FAT FAT Ambassadors: Anna Smith Higgs, Daisy Hollands, Emma Manderson, Frannie Carr, Georgia Hutton, Hannah Richards, Maisy Whipp, Nicola Haggett, Nicola Salmon, Rachel Smith, Sade Alexis

Katie is a facilitator, theatre maker and writer currently living in NE London. After graduating from East 15 Acting School with a degree in Acting and Community Theatre, Katie has been delivering projects and making work with young people and communities all over London – including at the Bush Theatre, the Roundhouse, The Yard and National Youth Theatre of GB.

Katie was a member of the Poetry Collective at the Roundhouse, as well as reaching the final of the Roundhouse Poetry Slam in 2018. She was a Resident Artist at the Roundhouse 2018-2019 and part of the Soho Theatre Writer's Lab programme. She has appeared on several podcasts, including *The Guilty Feminist* & *The Pleasure Podcast*, as well as writing for the *Metro*, *Refinery 29* & *Bustle*.

FATTY FAT FAT is her debut autobiographical solo show.

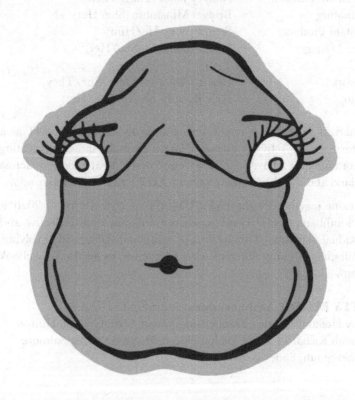

Author's Note:

A few years ago, I began to tell anecdotes from my life and when I reached – what I thought was – the punchline, I wasn't always met with the reaction I was expecting. Things I thought were 'normal' funny stories from growing up, I began to understand I was uniquely subject to because of being fat. Making *FATTY FAT FAT* was a way of reclaiming my fat body and its experiences in the world – and although it's based on my life, I hope it can do the same for you.

In spite of this, the heart of this show will always be a fat eighteen-year-old me trying to make friends at a party by telling funny stories from her childhood – so whilst there is heaviness, there is equally always a sense of fun. Likewise, the only 'bad guy' in the show is systemic fatphobia, driven by capitalism, rather than any individual people. I know that most people I've written about had good intentions – and I hope you can understand that too.

FATTY FAT FAT is an uprising. The show was created as both a revolution to (literally) take up the space nobody has ever wanted to give, and to pay homage to the fat activists whose work has allowed this show to exist. But before you get excited, *FATTY FAT FAT* isn't a utopia… yet. Instead it is beginning – rather than an end.

FATTY FAT FAT is for one performer of any age, gender or ethnicity.

The only thing that's important is that they are fat.

The house opens. The stage is bare apart from three silver helium balloons acting as plump platinum backdrop.

They unapologetically spell the word   FAT.

Beneath them stands **Katie.**

The Cha Cha Slide by DJ Casper is playing on repeat. **Katie** *is doing the prescribed routine over and over, interacting with the audience and encouraging them to join in. It is clear from this point that this show is not a 'conventional play'. This a celebration. A party. A show with a tangible sense of joy, nostalgia and tenderness.*

As the house closes **Katie** *is still going.*

She is still going.

The song is looping and **Katie** *is visibly tired & probably very sweaty. She probably makes a joke about being tired and sweaty. She softens the audience when she can – but never at her own expense. Regardless she appears to be enjoying herself.*

Eventually a projection appears behind her.

A picture of nine-year-old **Katie** *appears as music and lights fade.*

She stops dancing, takes everyone in and then begins.

Nine years old.

The Cha Cha Slide has just come out and it is a BANGER. I'd say it's in the top five party songs of all time.

One is the YMCA – obviously.
Two is the Macarena,
Three, I would say it's the Cha Cha Slide,

Four is Candy, (even though I never do it because I just feeling embarrassingly white),

And five is a curve ball. I think it's The Cheeky Girls song. Because I'm pretty sure that's how I learnt to move my hips, and that is a gift the world will forever be grateful for.

Have I missed any?

Katie *encourages the audience to offer suggestions. Actual suggestions, even if they don't want to.* **Katie** *reacts and interacts with them. Someone seems to always mention 'Saturday Night' much to* **Katie's** *delight.*

I like a song with a set routine. So another classic is Oops Upside Your Head. An absolute banger because it combines two of my favourite things: dancing…and sitting down.

Anyway, I digress. I've just got my first Walkman and so CDs are like all I want right now. I spend hours delving through the bargain bucket of Woolworths building up what I'm sure is going to be a *hugely* valuable collection. One day, my mum picks me up from school, she asks me the classic questions:

'How was your day?'
 and
'What did you have for lunch?',

before saying there's a present for me in her handbag.

My pudgy fingers delve excited into the coloured leather of her handbag, dancing around her lip gloss and Nokia until they feel the familiar plastic of a CD case.

Pause.

The Cha Cha fucking Slide!

I thank her enthusiastically, already imagining the jealous grimace on my ex-best friend Lauren Chaffyn's face tomorrow morning.

'You're welcome,' my Mum says.

'I thought you could put it in your Walkman and use it as an exercise tape.'

Cha Cha Slide ends.

Another picture of **Katie** *appears, this time at five years old, as music and lights fade.*

The Thomas the Tank Engine Theme plays loudly. After a few seconds it fades to a volume that can be spoken over

Five years old.

It's World Book Day, and my mum has taken a long time over my costume. Three of the girls in my class are Pippi Longstocking, with wired plaits and stripy socks that refuse to stay up.

But I am feeling *majestic* because I have been chosen by Mrs Wells as the best dressed, not just in my class, but the WHOLE YEAR. So I sashay across the muddy lino in the school hall, leaving Spot the Dogs and Hermione Grangers in my wake- because I know today I reign supreme.

We sit in our neat rows, my costume is not comfortable to sit cross legged in, but despite being five years old I am acutely aware that one must suffer for one's *art.*

Mrs Hitchcock, the Headteacher, invites the winners of each year group to stand up, show their costume and announce who they are to the whole school.

The little girl from Reception is clearly cute, but her Alice in Wonderland costume is missing attention to detail. The boy from year 1's handmade cardboard dinosaur is impressive, but his face paint is already smudged with his own spit.

Then it's my turn.

I rise proudly from the mass of cheap wigs and cuddly toys, standing regally in everyone's expectant gaze.

Then I repeat, just like my mother told me...

'I am dressed as the Fat Controller from Thomas the Tank Engine.'

Thomas the Tank Engine Theme ends.

Eleven years old.

We're sat in Mum's blue Honda CR-V, listening to Radio 2. Like we always do. Except its Jeremy Vine time and he's just argumentative and shit. This doesn't help my mood, some classic easy listening tunes, are more what I'm looking for this afternoon. Well, let's be honest I'd rather listen to Natasha Bedingfield because her latest song is a TUNE.

It's summer so the sunroof is open, I feel the fresh air of the M27 stroke my hair and I rest my hand in my mum's.
It's not dangerous because she drives an automatic, so she doesn't need it anyway.

Holding my mum's hand always calms me down. Our fingers interlock like a lifeboat, stopping us both from sinking and I need it today because I am feeling a little bit nervous.
Because I am about to be hypnotised – by mum's friend Karen from the tennis club.

Now apart from this lady swinging a watch in front of my face, I don't really know what to expect. All I know is that I'm about to be hypnotised to stop me being fat.

And to stop biting my nails.

But mainly the fat thing.

The picture disappears as music fades to silence.

The picture disappears as the Price is Right Theme tune loudly interrupts any sense of sentimentality. **Katie** *adorns herself with an extravagant sequin coat and comes centre stage. It should feel like we're 'On Air' all of a sudden.*

Ladies, gentleman, non-binaries and fellow gender queers, welcome to The Size is Right – with me your host Katarina Green. How is everyone tonight? Who's feeling lucky?

There's lots of encouraged cheers and applause.

Before we get started let me first remind you of the rules of the Size is Right. The key is not to be too small or too big but "The Right Size"!

What is it everyone?

They repeat "The Right Size" back to her.

Tonight, we are playing for an amazing money-can't-buy prize! Which is… drum roll please… FREEDOM FROM THE CLUTCHES OF SYSTEMIC FATPHOBIA!

A huge round of applause.

Now we've had contestants from all over the country, from Land's End to John O'Groats and everywhere in between. Have we got anyone in from further afield today?

Answers are taken from the audience and riffed off in a traditional game show fashion, every place is made to seem more exciting than the next.

Now to find out who's going to be our lucky contestant tonight, we'll be picking our contestant in the traditional Size is Right fashion.

(part sing-a-long, part catchphrase)

Put your hands up high,
Now down below,
Between your legs,
Who's on the show?

The audience root around until one of them finds a pack of crisps taped to the underside of their seat. The winner is invited down to the stage to rapturous applause.

What's your name? Where have you come from this evening?

Katie *ad-libs with the contestant.*

Okay, so I am going to ask you a series of questions and you have to decide whether or not the answer is higher or lower than the number given. And hopefully you'll win tonight's grand prize! Does that make sense?

It probably doesn't – and that's okay, **Katie** *carries on anyway.*

It's time to get started! Our first round is a classic. So, how many standard size pencils can I fit under my left breast?

Our starting number is five. Now audience do you think it's higher or lower than five?

The audience say 'higher' or 'lower'.

So, which do you think?

The contestant makes a choice.

Let's find out if you're right…

A sound indicating whether or not the answer is right or wrong is heard.

And the answer is higher it's…nine.

This is met with either congratulations or commiserations.

The next one is a little bit more unconventional. Whilst squatting how many teaspoons can I hold between my abdomen and thighs? Let me demonstrate.

Katie *squats and gestures to the area in question. It looks slightly odd and definitely uncomfortable.*

Now audience do you think it's higher or lower than nine?

The audience say 'higher' or 'lower'.

The contestant makes a choice.

Let's find out if you're right…

A sound indicating whether or not the answer is right or wrong is heard.

And the answer is lower. A close one, it's eight.

This is met with either congratulations or commiserations.

Now this is a key round, before we get to the all-important final one. How many lipsticks can I fully conceal in my stomach rolls whilst seated? Now audience, do you think it's higher or lower than eight?

The audience say 'higher' or 'lower.

The contestant makes a choice.

Let's find out if you're right…

A sound indicating whether or not the answer is right or wrong is heard.

And the answer is six.

Met with either congratulations or commiserations. Regardless of how they've 'scored' the next round is offered.

Now this is the last round. This is where it all gets exciting!

Okay, our final winner-takes-all round, is a live one. This will determine if you go home with tonight's amazing prize... FREEDOM FROM THE CLUTCHES OF SYSTEMIC FATPHOBIA!

Now, I need you to predict how many Skittles can I hold under my chins. I need you to make a guess and whisper it in the ear of my independent adjudicator, sat right here (*Indicates to someone sat on the front row.*) whilst I prepare.

The contestant makes their guess whilst the packet of Skittles is retrieved.

Has the guess been independently verified?

Adjudicator confirms.

Then I shall begin, count with me everyone!

Katie *places skittles one by one under her chin(s). The audience counts along. As soon as one falls, the game is over. It's surprisingly tense and captivating.*

Now what was the guess?

The adjudicator confirms the contestant's guess.

There is celebration or commiseration. The contestant is thanked, before returning to their seat.

Thank you so much for joining me for The Size is Right! I have been your host Katerina Green – goodnight!

Katie *takes a long bow and begins to remove her coat. As she does, she challenges the audience with her gaze.*

*The following text is recorded whilst **Katie** is moving for the duration.*
Beneath the text is a delicate but sprawling underscore.

Whilst the text is playing, her body ripples across the stage very loosely
mimicking the action of washing her body. It is a graceful version of
something deliberately undignified. A dance of something deeply functional,
and unique to each body and its owner.

Throughout the section the movement softens and intensifies in response to
the text.

I had one bath, last year, that I actually enjoyed. Which is a
100% increase on the last five years. Although I'm too big for
the ceramic womb, I fit perfectly. An echo chamber of fat golden
flesh tucked into itself.

Flesh rolled into flesh rolled into flesh rolled into...

The taps are blocked by myself. A plug of pink, a wad of
something soft and warm that I call home. Precious ripples
of me, expanding into mountains that rise proudly from her
fragrant sea. We hold each other equal in our care. Wholesome
and *nearly* loving.

I wish I could bathe in celebration. That I could anoint my body
in wonder. But instead I douse it in vengeful stares and lusty
grasps – practising pulling bits of me away from myself.

Since I first wrote this show two new clusters of stretch marks
have formed under each of my breasts. Red tears from where
my body couldn't keep the sadness in. Cities of sorrow collected
under bags of wasted motherhood.

I look in the mirror and apologise for hating them. But I can't
help but see wiggles of betrayal on my chest.

The red cracks used to be confined to my stomach, but they have
broken out of their quarantine, and now crawl across my torso
leaving reminders of where my even my skin couldn't take it
anymore.

I stand on this stage with scars emblazoned on a body, that is
also telling you they shouldn't matter, which makes the shame
shatter tighter across my chest. That is why this show can't be
celebration – yet.

Just a quest to understand.

The atmosphere settles but something has shifted.

A picture appears. This time it's **Katie** *at ten years old. Smile by Lily Allen plays loudly. After a few seconds it fades to a volume that can be spoken over.*

Ten years old.

It's hot outside, but I wish it wasn't. When it's warm I feel obliged to make the most of the weather, when really, I just feel like staying inside and watching TV.

It's hard being ten – there's lots going on.

My dad is mowing the lawn and my mother is weeding- everyone is in their classic weekend stations. To ensure optimum comfort whilst watching CBBC, I recline, placing both my legs on the arm of the sofa. As I do, I notice this sort of puckering of my skin.

(I had already watched this episode of Arthur so I figured I'd investigate my own thigh instead).

This small section of skin looks like the surface of the moon, covered in bumps and crevices. I roll my leg across the sofas much bigger one, chasing my own skin.

I was sure I had made an important discovery so I ran outside to share it with my mum, as I was sure she was going to be as excited as me. Her face was buried in a rose bush as I approached her, so I grabbed a handful of my galactic thigh and showed it to her.

'Look at this mum, my skin is loose, it must be because I've lost weight'.

She replies

        'No, that's just cellulite'.

Smile ends.

The next picture appears of **Katie** *at nineteen years old as All About That Bass by Meghan Trainor plays loudly. After a few seconds it fades to a volume that can be spoken over.*

Nineteen years old.

We're in my favourite Thai restaurant – my aunt, her friend Anne and me. We make polite conversation over noodles and vegetables. Well, let's be honest, I have my own Pad Thai and they're sharing sides – because that's all they could possibly manage.

I call bullshit, but anyway.

Anne's nephew went to the Royal Central School of Speech and Drama. He's doing terribly well as an actor. And as a director. And pretty much smashing life altogether. GOOD FOR YOU ANNE'S NEPHEW.

Then conversation turns to me.

'What's sort of acting would you like to do Katie?'

'Well to be honest, Anne I don't really want to be a jobbing actor. I'm more interested in Community Theatre, Participatory Theatre, or maybe even making my own work.'

'Oh, don't be silly Katie, of course you can be an actor! There are plenty of actors that look like you'.

Which is when my aunt chimes in and says,

'Yes, you'd make an excellent chamber maid in Downton Abbey.'

And Anne finishes off by saying

'Yes, don't let your weight stop you from following your dreams.'

Sorry Anne, I didn't actually realise I was.

All About That Bass ends.

*Similarly, to earlier, this text is recorded whilst **Katie** moves across the stage. This time she is seen sitting down, crossing her legs and then getting back up. Initially this is rushed, yet enthusiastic. A lot of flesh folding into itself and then flung back out again – like trying to pack away a pop-up tent.*

As she repeats the action you see the pain and fatigue grow in her body. You see the precision and planning behind this task, you see the effort it takes. By the end she is slow and suffering – but in spite of this, she keeps going.

I teach musical theatre to three year olds on a Saturday morning.
The children burst into the class with a playful stumble.
Legs, lines and elbows tumbling. Their bodies are infinite
with possibilities. They bounce and dance and wiggles with a
freedom, I can't remember.
All my memories seem to be tainted with the mark of loathing,
before I really knew what it was.
I fold my big body next to theirs – forcing my legs into a cross.
Unlike the journey here, everyone is in a rush to sit next to me.
Legs, lines and elbows somehow smoothing out their edges to
make a circle. I ask everyone to reach out and touch their toes
– knowing that for me, I relinquished that power decades ago.
Then, from nowhere, I feel two soft limpet hands next to me, as
she pulls with all her might so that the poles in my palms and
toes can meet. And she won't let go until she sees me do it.
And it's only afterwards, I appreciate the value of the care she
takes over my body. Without thought or judgement, she takes
her tearstained fingers and intertwines them in the hairs of
my forearms – with the sole instinct to help. Instead of touches
from fingers tainted with hurting, she anoints my skin with snot
covered care.

A picture of **Katie** *aged twenty-two edges in, whilst Youth by Daughter plays loudly. After a few seconds it fades to a volume that can be spoken over.*

This story feels different to the ones we've heard so far, despite it being set up in the same way. It's almost like **Katie** *might not want to tell it.*

Twenty-two years old.

I am lying naked next to the first person that broke my heart.

My fingers are dancing over the galaxies of her forearms, whilst our soft bodies sink into the even softer bed clothes.

She rolls over. Her bum fits perfectly into the gap between my thighs and breasts. I tell her that other than her lips and fingertips, this is my favourite part of her. Her shoulders dance with the predictability of my declaration and a giggle wiggles across my cheeks, as I feel her turn back towards me.

'This is my favourite part of you,' she says, as she places those precious fingertips on my milky white tummy.

And so, for the first time I wished my stomach was bigger.

That it was so *vast* that it would make up for all the other ways in which I was never enough for her.

A picture of **Katie** *at twenty-one years old appears as Talk Dirty by Jason Derulo plays loudly. After a few seconds it fades to a volume that can be spoken over.*

Twenty-one years old.

I am leaving Talk nightclub, aka the sweetcorn kernel in the pile of shit that's Southend's night-time 'scene' – but it's free party Friday, so where else would I be?

I was on the pull. As usual.
And was unsuccessful. As usual.

But seeing as I have to run a youth theatre in under five hours, I figure it's time to call it a night.

As I exit, I shimmy my way past some commotion at the door. As I said, it's 3:30am on Free Party Friday, in Southend so I'm hardly surprised. But as I stagger past I hear a woman using really gross slurs towards the bouncer who won't let her in.

Now he won't let her in because it's past last entry. So rather than going home or making other plans, she's chosen to be an outright racist dickhead instead. Now I've had enough drinks that I feel brave – but not so many that I don't know what I'm doing – so I flick my hair and say,

(Slightly slurred.) 'Stop being a fucking racist, this guy is just trying to do his job – please go home!'

She is silent, so I nod at the bouncer and stagger triumphant in my moral victory, across the sick speckled car park and into the horizon.

But then I hear her shout at me. My too bare skin seems to shrink around my bones.

'At least I don't have backrolls,' she says.

The picture disappears as the music throbs, before fading to silence.

Katie is snapped out of the moment by The Nutcracker, Op.71: Act II
Tableau 3: Variation 2: Dance of the Sugar Plum Fairy.

Katie moves forward, centre stage. She does some pointless stretches and
vocal trills. She exits and re-enters with a pair of jeans.

In time with the flutters of music she attempts to wrestle them on. She falls
on the floor, rolls and jumps. It's funny – almost clown-like but you can
occasionally catch the shame seeping out through the gaps in her smile.

It's part ballet, part battle cry.
Eventually she gets the jeans on. Just. But she quickly realises how
unflattering they are and rips them off, getting stuck and trapped in a cheap
denim hell. In time with the song ending **Katie** breaks free and throws
them to the ground.

She is triggered, yet triumphant. For now at least.

Sk8er Boi by Avril Lavigne erupts loudly as a picture of **Katie** *aged seven appears. After a few seconds it fades to a volume that can be spoken over.*

Seven years old.

It's maths in Mrs Tarlton's class. I feel like there's some tension in the air today, for two reasons:

 1. I'm wearing my new green hairband and it's super cool. I think some people might be jealous.

2. I am the reigning and unbeaten champion at Times Table shootout and I can feel people coming for me. I think it's the age seven equivalent of being on the run.

Mrs Tarlton asks Katy Matthews to hand out the textbooks. We all know the power the textbook hander-outer-er yields, so I admire her longingly as she skips across the crunchy carpet. When she gets to me, I hold out my hands expectantly.

She chucks the book across my desk and says,

'Here you go. Also, you're fat'. *(The music stops.)*

Now this does not sit well with me, so I march to the front of the class. And whilst framed by the whiteboard I say,

'Katy M just called me fat, so everyone come and sit on the carpet in a circle and listen to her apologise to me.'

She did. No one ever called me fat at school after that.

Not to my face anyway.

Sk8er Boi Ends.

Katie *stands centre stage as the following recorded text begins to play. She is stood beneath the balloons spelling out FAT. At first, she is just listening with the audience to the words, then she begins to gently interact with her body.*

Initially this action is soft touches and pokes, but this gradually intensifies. She moves from stroking to pinching to punching almost without you noticing. It builds into a battle with her body using the words as ammunition. Her own power pushes her body across the stage, ricocheting between the audience's stares. It is repetitive and almost ritualistic – a fit of frustration and flesh.

Her fists pummel into her bulbous body until it's too much. It ends with **Katie** *having no choice but to hold herself.*

It's mad to think it was only about a year ago I began to call myself fat, and now here I am stood underneath a set of balloons spelling it right out. A platinum covered pledge, that I could be ok with it all.

FAT is still a word that fizzes on my tongue like a parma violet; sickly and sweet and even though you're not sure if you like it, you just carry on eating it anyway. It rattles round my gums and rots my teeth, with a weight I think I'm beginning to enjoy.

F   A   T

The F is full of fighting. Tears and shouting, all the times my body was a reason and an excuse. Blown tight with promises to change. The A is the apologies. Seams sticky with sorrys from when I couldn't deflate, no matter how much I wanted too. And T is torment that I couldn't change it. That I am bound in something that grew to be broken.

But FAT fits better than big or curvy or bubbly. It hugs me tighter than chubby, plump or larger, but doesn't wrap its vowels around my throat like *obese* does. This show began as a whisper of retrieval, trying to sink my fingers back into a body that has been snatched from me, but in doing that I've had to relinquish the right to decide what words people use about me and my body.

Every time I perform this show it is painful. My soft stories become funny, because that's the only way I know how to tell them. Your laughter and applause wrap around my pudgy limbs like armour.

Which I need to hold onto tightly because this show feels like a beginning, not an end.

Katie *moves forward, centre stage. Lights up. Doctor's Orders by Jane McDonald plays.*

Have we got any performers in the house?

She prods, pokes and persuades until she finds a volunteer.

Great, come on down!

You are a doctor. Think about your doctor name and backstory – think about your wants, needs, desires. Great. I know a lot of people in tonight so please don't make me look bad. You just need to read these cards and be the doctor. Can you do that?

You need to wear this. According to Amazon it's what a Doctor wears.

*Gives audience member slightly weird costume which consists of a nurse's headband, stethoscope and garter with a syringe pen attached to it. The audience member puts it on as best as they can. Lastly **Katie** hands them their script for the scene.*

Ready to go? Lights, Camera Action!

Dr: Hello Katherine, how are you doing?

Katie: Hello Doctor!

Dr: What can I help you with today?

Katie: I cut my hand last week on a rusty can and it's gone a little yellow and smelly. Silly me!

Dr: That's not very good. Can I take your blood pressure?

Katie:	Oh okay…
Dr:	*Mimes taking blood pressure.*
Katie:	I wasn't sure if it was worth bothering you about but a friend of mine said I should come and see you as the cut looked rather alarming.
Dr:	Hmmm.
Katie:	Is it not good news Doctor?
Dr:	No, but it's very surprising. Your blood pressure is perfectly normal.
Katie:	Surely that's a good thing?
Dr:	It's not what we'd expect of someone like you. Anyway, a blood test!
Katie:	Ah yes, you'll have to bear with me – I'm not that good with needles!
Dr:	You must be used to them by now because of your diabetes and all those insulin shots.
Katie:	Am I diabetic doctor?
Dr:	Oh sorry, I presumed. Your BMI puts you at risk of type 2 diabetes.
Katie:	Yes. Right. Okay.
	But what about the hand, my fingers really are starting to tingle!

Dr: So what weight loss methods have you tried so far?

Katie: I gave up crisps for Lent once… but I generally eat pretty well

Dr: I've heard Slimming World is popular at the moment.

Katie: Yes, I've seen the adverts, they're everywhere. But I also know that statically only 5% of people keep the weight off for more than five years.

Dr: You should consider weight loss surgery. It's popular for those looking for a quick and easy fix.

Katie: Yes, I guess I can think about it but they can have some terrible risks… like *death*.

Dr: As you are morbidly obese, I have just recommended you for the weight loss scheme run by the local council.

Katie: But it's my hand I'm here for. Can you prescribe me some ANYTHING?

Dr: We're actually out of time. The NHS is so stretched these days. Give us a call in a week to hear about your diabetes test results. Bye!

Audience member returns to seat. It's kind of awkward but **Katie** *enjoys it. This is broken quickly by the next song.*

A picture of twenty-three year old **Katie** *materialises, as Gotta Get Thru This by Daniel Bedingfield plays loudly. After a few seconds it fades to a volume that can be spoken over.*

Twenty-three years old.

I am on the 36 bus from Camberwell to Vauxhall as part of my mid-day commute. I am eating my lunch – some delicious pesto pasta – out of a Lidl yogurt bucket recycled as a Tupperware.

I cleverly forgot a fork, so I instead I am using three fingers as a shovel. My very own carb-y bucket and spade.

As my basil seasoned fingered are beavering away I see and older man staring at me whilst I eat. This is unpleasant but not unusual, the constant but often unavoidable peril of eating in public.

These days I have my green eyes circulating rooms, carriages and open spaces ready to silently stare anyone down who dares approach me. I'm already composing my semi-viral tweet calling out this man's fatphobia, when I hear him speak to me.

'Give me your Tupperware.'

'Excuse me?' I reply

'I've been waiting for you to finish. I know exactly what I'm going to use it for.'

'But it's… mine. I was going to use it again?', but by this point the whole bottom deck was staring. He opens his crispy back for life expectantly and says,

'I'm getting off at the next stop, I was going to ask you to hurry up.'

The bus pulls up and so I'm out of time, so I place my
Tupperware – by it's very useful handle – into the bag.

He hobbles off the bus and says,

'Every time I use it, I'll remember you.'

And then I never saw my beloved Tupperware again.

Gotta Get Thru This ends

We hear the final piece of recorded text whilst **Katie** *moves around the stage playfully with a smile aching in her cheeks. Her actions begin big, floaty and indulgent before softening into her own fingers skating across her body.*

Initially she watches them, each moment loaded with remembering. Gradually **Katie** *becomes disconnected from the audience. The movements gradually shrink and lose precision, so by the end they've dissolved into nothingness. By the end we seem to have lost* **Katie** *to herself.*

This summer, I did something incredibly creatively unstimulating and fell in love. The nights of profoundly poetic and seemingly perpetual heartbreak ended – just like that. So instead the summer was littered with buttery crumbs of laughter and lying belly side up on bed frames.

Mornings become meringues, crunchy until they hit the tongue dissolving into a sweet whisper. And as the nights start to get longer, somewhere between the Chicken Kievs and spikey teardrops we still fall asleep holding hands.

We start to shed the sweet honeymoon. After kisses in the boardroom we console our evening by adopting a kilo's worth of toad in the hole. Staring at you with arms full of food is my favourite view.

Your cauliflower cheese lips meet in an apology after some top deck angst. We curl into mash potato kisses until we are full of each other. Busting with something I'd never before been able to truly satisfy.

Until now hunger was the only love I taught my body to understand. And when you've fed yourself loneliness for a lifetime it's hard to imagine ever being full.

My arteries are filled with the treacle rhetoric of having to love yourself before loving somebody else. As I stand there with handfuls of leftover flesh, I feel guilty that my hatred takes up space that instead could be full of you.

A picture of **Katie** *aged thirteen eventually appears as When I Grow Up by The Pussycat Dolls plays loudly. After a few seconds it fades to a volume that can be spoken over.*

Thirteen years old.

Every summer there always a project, not just from school but a personal one. It was always the same, but often had slightly different wording. This year my mother cut straight to the point.

This summer was the summer I would lose weight.

The scales are kept outside my room, like they always have been. The amount of times I've stubbed my toes on them in the dark or woken to click of them in morning. You're always a few pounds lighter in the morning and I needed all the help I could get so we would start tomorrow.

The ridged plastic felt like it was burning my feet, as the red neon lines wrote my fate in lights. She wrote it in her best fountain pen. The ink licked the pages, like my tongue licked the tears from my cheeks.
We had work to do.

As I was thirteen I could finally go to the gym alone, so I was given a session with a personal trainer to devise a regime I could implement myself. I used to go on the rowing machine, although my arms weren't long enough to reach the bar thing.

I did my best though.

And now I can see my mum was just trying to *her* best too.

When I Grow Up ends.

Katie *moves towards the audience. She is ready to play.*

Right so now we're going to play one last game altogether. As it's my show I can do whatever I like and so we're going to play one of my favourite games… Never Have I Ever.

Now normally you play this with drinks, but instead I think I've got something, in my opinion, better… CRISPS. And this is where I get my Oprah moment!

Crisps are thrown out randomly into the audience. It's chaotic, colourful and carb-y. **Katie** *ad-libs as they're thrown, facilitating swaps of flavours and ensuring as many people as possible have a packet. It's fun as people scrabble around and feels a bit like a childrens' disco.*

Some people always, and inevitably, start eating.

Right, did I say you could start? When someone gives you a gift do you just open it? No, I didn't think so. It's not just a snack to get you through the last bit of the show, it's a device!
The rules are a track is going to play, and like normal Never Have I Ever, whenever you hear a statement that is true for you, you eat a crisp.

Got it? Okay let's play!

Katie *moves centre stage and the recorded text begins.*

She listens and begins eating more causally, much like the majority of the audience, occasionally reacting to what she's heard.

The game is fun – and more importantly delicious.

As the track continues the statements get faster, as does **Katie***'s eating. It gradually becomes grotesque and by the end she is stuffing her face, crisp crumbs pouring out of her mouth. It is uncomfortable to watch* **Katie** *literally pour salt into her wounds.*

Some members of the audience will stop eating when we see her struggling.
Some will always keep going.

Never Have I Ever eaten more carbs than vegetables in a week.

Never Have I Ever had clothes fit my arse but not my waist.

Never Have I Ever eaten way more than three meals in a day.

Never Have I Ever bought a pair of trousers too small as an incentive to lose weight.

Never Have I Ever experienced that moment of panic in a changing room when you get trapped in a piece of clothing that's too small.

Never Have I Ever eaten food off a stranger's plate.

Never Have I Ever gone to find clothes in a shop and not been able to find anything that fits, that's not like ugly or black.

Never Have I Ever had to get off a roller coaster because the safety harness wouldn't fit.

Never Have I Ever had your thighs clap together so loud people thought you'd farted.

Never Have I Ever been offered to borrow clothes by a thin friend and wondered if they were nice, blind or stupid.

Never Have I Ever been compared to Adele or Dawn French because they're the only fat celebrities people can think of.

Never Have I Ever had to make a joke about my size in order to make other people feel more comfortable.

Never Have I Ever made sure I included a full body picture or an unflattering photo in an online dating profile, to make sure I'm not an unwelcome surprise

Never Have I Ever had to use a towel that was barely able to wrap round my arms, let alone my body. And then like accidentally flashed a stranger.

Never Have I Ever felt full of dread approaching a chair with arms and wondering whether or not I'll actually fit in it.

Never Have I Ever been mistaken for the other fat person in the room/group even though the only thing that is remotely similar about us is we're fat.

Never Have I Ever been told I have a 'pretty face' and found it deeply offensive as I know its code for something else.

Never Have I Ever had restaurant touts fight over getting me in their establishment, because they assume I'm going to rack up the biggest bill.

Never Have I Ever not been able to change my tampon because the toilet cubicle was so small I couldn't separate my thighs.

Never Have I Ever had a double seat to myself on public transport because people don't want to sit next to me. Even when it's packed.

Never Have I Ever been told I was brave just for wearing a piece of clothing.

Never Have I Ever had strangers comment on food I'm eating in public.

Never Have I Ever been offered money to lose weight.

Never Have I Ever had someone actively deny kissing me because they are ashamed.

Never Have I Ever fallen down in public and been laughed at rather than helped.

Never Have I Ever been called a 'fat bitch' by random passers-by.

Never Have I Ever been noticeably the fattest person in a room.

Silence.

Katie *is covered in crisps, so is the floor beneath her and her mouth can barely shut. She has no choice but to finish what she's started, so she continues to try and chew and swallow in the silence.*

It takes a while.

Sometimes it takes ages.

She chews and swallows until it is bearable again – for now at least.

Eventually the moment is broken and we return to the party-like atmosphere we recognise.

We see the final picture of **Katie** *at seventeen years old as Waiting All Night by Rudimental and Ella Eyre plays loudly. It doesn't have a chance to get loud as it is spoken over immediately.*

Something is coming.

Seventeen years old.

It's Saturday night in the centre of all life – aka The Wetherspoons in Salisbury. I've managed to get in using a girl in the year above me's ID – she's currently got a fractured ankle, so I'm renting it off her. I'm at the bar wrestling my too short skirt down my thighs, desperately trying to catch the barman's eye but he's not looking at me. Finally, I order two pitchers, both for me.

I struggle up the stairs. For a moment everyone is excited to see me because they think the drinks are to share, but once they realise they're not normal conversation ensues. We talk about our route through town, other girls in our year and boys – all tinged with a familiar tone of desperation. After multiple loo trips, someone being sick and a couple of nip slips, we're ready to head to our first destination.

We stumble through the cobbles, the dark shadow of the Cathedral Spire sharper than our smudged eyeliner.

After a round of jäger-bombs and an awkward dance, we decide to move on to avoid being caught on the light-up dance floor next to someone's ex boyfriend's sister.

Then we head to White Rooms. Now White Rooms is literally couple of white rooms, full of white people, but they are playing my song and I'm happy.

Growing up fat meant that literally no boy our age fancied me. And I went to an all-girls school which meant I only really knew about ten boys anyway – which made it worse when none of them fancied me. And my friends were great, always bringing me along to stuff. But I was never explicitly invited to the parties and I think that was because no one wanted to be associated with the fat girl. And to be fair, I didn't really want to be associated with her either but I didn't really have a choice.

But once we started going out into the big lights of Salisbury town, I realised there was a whole bunch of Squaddies and Middle-aged Men I could tap into. I'd dance in my too short skirt until my feet hurt. Breasts squished into bright coloured bras, reflecting the slowly blushing skies of morning.

Tonight, I see this group checking me out, they whisper and giggle as I wiggle my arse in their direction. They nudge each other forward, each more reluctant than each other until one high-fives his way to victory.

We dance, like our bodies don't fit and my friends smile as he licks his lips and leans in. His lips taste fizzy, as our tongues struggle for space in the spin cycle.

After a moment, I see we are surrounded by the most mediocre paparazzi, a circle of Blackberrys taking pictures of us. Of me. Their jeer sounds like a seal being run over so I pull away.

He is met by pats on the back, a pint and a fiver – because he won the bet and kissed me. To my friends I was a hero, and even cooler for turning him down. They don't get it, because they don't ever have to.

So, I just keep dancing.

Music comes on very loud as we hear the bridge of the song building. There's a sense of anticipation as she plays with her clothes, maybe even removing a top layer.

Then she starts to dance.

The movement just roars out of her — she is ready for battle.

She's spinning and moving and we see flickers of earlier movements reappear. Everything has built to this moment. There is a crescendo of flesh but as it's about to erupt **Katie** *yells to stop the music, just after the beat has dropped. Unwelcome silence. The house lights are on.*

It's too bright. It's too quiet.

We can finally see **Katie** *properly, for what we now realise is the first time. She's looking right at you in a way she's been avoiding. The stage feels really empty. She looks small, sweaty and exposed.*

And this is the moment where I was going to dance and take off all my clothes, to show that I don't give a fuck. And genuinely over the time I've been developing this show I've changed my mind about a hundred times about what I was going to do. I felt like I had to be at peace with my body for this show to be valid- and the only way I could do that was to be naked to show I was ok with it all. But, I was so terrified of the prospect of doing that, that I nearly didn't make the show at all.
Because as long as I live in this fat body, I will constantly seek validation from everyone other than myself for its existence.

Katie *sings the chorus of Waiting All Night acapella. Her voice is taut with hurting.*

'I've been waiting all night for you to
Tell me what you want
Tell me,
Tell me that you need me'

But what I really want is my body back.

I'm not the spokesperson of Fatness. These are some of my experiences in my body. A body that is exceptionally privileged because it is white, cis-gendered, middle class, able bodied and 'small fat'. I want you to understand the fat experience is so much bigger than me.

I want charities, businesses and people to stop using my body as a scapegoat – regardless of the cause. My fat is not something you can villainize me for but then just roll out when it suits you. I want my health not to feel like a burden. That rather than the Tories, Richard Branson or greed – my folds are the reason our NHS is folding.

I want to stop wishing every night before I go to sleep that I'll wake up in the morning thinner.

I want to not be ashamed of my body – be braver than the hisses from your hallowed cheeks, instead, I want to listen to the echo chamber I've created on my feeds.

When children I work sink their fingers into my stomach, questioning. I want to tell them I am fat and to be proud of that.

I want to not have to think about what I wear. Not worry about the colours or the contour my body makes. I want fabric to frame my rolls like a masterpiece not hide them in a vault of dark polyester.

I want my boobs not to be used as a distraction or redeeming feature. A mound of flesh literally defending people's gaze from my gut. Instead I want to be able to strap them down and still feel sexy.

And I want to online date and not be scared of being fatter in person, so much so I've even written it in my bio.

Then I want to sit on someone's face without the fear of squashing them.

And when that's a disaster, I want to not have to settle because I feel lucky to have found someone.

Anyone.

I want people to laugh when my thighs clap down the stairs, because my body is an orchestra – its symphony harmonises with your laughter.

I want to travel without the dread the seatbelt won't fit or the armrest having to ascend too. I want my body not to be a tourist attraction of its own. Instead I want it to be treated like the eighth Wonder of the World.

I want to be able to eat on public transport. I want to dust crisp crumbs off my thighs without the flutter of sighs loaded with micro-aggression.

And I want to stand with my arms by my side and not crossed over my body. Physically screwing myself up so I take up less room. Flesh concertinaed into a squeeze box of shame.

I want to feed my body when it's hungry. When my soft stomach cries I want to hold it and feed it with something other than itself.

I want to be quiet and small. Not have to fill the room with my cultivated personality to overshadow the space my body takes up.

I want to be beautiful because I'm fat not in spite of it.

I want to stop judging people the way they judged me.

I want to not feel betrayed by my body because everyone's told me I should be.

I want you to understand that me calling myself fat, doesn't give you the right to.

I just want to walk down the street in my body and for it not be political.

I want my body back.

Blackout.

END

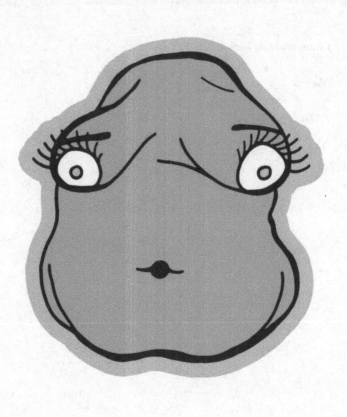

THE BEGINNINGS OF
THE FAT ACCEPTANCE MOVEMENT

The Fat Acceptance movement started in the 1960s which aimed to tackle anti-fat bias in society by raising awareness of discrimination directed towards people in higher weight bodies. It began as a movement to create a space where bodies rejected by society could exist. A place where bodies that didn't fit the conventional mould could come together to celebrate, learn from, and support each other – essentially to create a subculture separate from the one they'd been rejected from.

In 1972 the Fat Underground was formed and the name was chosen as its initials expressed the group's sentiments. The group took issue with what they saw as a growing bias against 'obesity' in the scientific community and acted as a catalyst in the conception and mobilisation of the Fat Liberation movement. Rather than seeking to change discriminatory laws, the group focused on challenging discriminatory thoughts and practices across different aspects of society. They were inspired by the Radical Therapy Collective, a group that believed people with mental illness were not to carry the burden of changing themselves, but instead the focus should be placed on changing the societal stigma surrounding it. As a result, the 'change society, not ourselves' ideology underpinned much of the activism in the Fat Liberation Movement.

The group were criticised initially by academics, colleagues and other early fat activists, particularly members of the National Association to Advance Fat Acceptance (NAAFA), for being 'too aggressive'. However, ultimately many of these people came to adopt much of the Fat Underground's ideas in their respective fields. In November 1973, Judy Freespirit and Aldebran published the "Fat Liberation Manifesto" on behalf of the Fat Underground. This manifesto outlines the aims and ambitions of the group and ends in a call to action. This was a key turning point as it one of the first times there was a public call for fat people to unite for a cause.

Since then the fat acceptance and activist movement has had a rich history across the world. More recently it has been seen to be co-opted and commodified by 'Body Positivity'. However, it's important to remember that fat acceptance is anti-capitalist activist movement at its core. Although there has been significant progress in the last decades, the fight is definitely far from over.

FAT LIBERATION MANIFESTO
BY JUDY FREESPIRIT AND ALDEBARAN
NOVEMBER 1973

1. We believe that fat people are fully entitled to human respect and recognition.

2. We are angry at mistreatment by commercial and sexist interests. These have exploited our bodies as objects of ridicule, thereby creating an immensely profitable market selling the false promise of avoidance of, or relief from, that ridicule.

3. We see our struggle as allied with the struggles of other oppressed groups, against classism, racism, sexism, ageism, capitalism, imperialism, and the like.

4. We demand equal rights for fat people in all aspects of life, as promised in the Constitution of the United States. We demand equal access to goods and services in the public domain, and an end to discrimination against us in the areas of employment, education, public facilities and health services.

5. We single out as our special enemies that so-called "reducing" industries. These include diet clubs, reducing salons, fat farms, diet doctors, diet books, diet foods and food supplements surgical procedures, appetite suppressants, drug and gadgetry such as wraps and "reducing machines".

6. We demand that they take responsibility for their false claims, acknowledge that their products are harmful to the public health, and publish long-term studies proving any statistical efficacy of their products. We make this demand knowing that over 99% of all weight loss programs, when evaluated over a five-year period, fail utterly, and also knowing the extreme, proven harmfulness of repeated large changes in weight.

7. We repudiate the mystified "science" which falsely claims that we are unfit. It as both caused and upheld discrimination against us, in collusion with the financial interests of insurance companies, the fashion and garment industries, reducing industries, the food and drug establishments.

8. We refuse to be subjected to the interests of our enemies. We fully intend to reclaim power over our bodies and lives. We commit ourselves to pursue these goals together.

FAT PEOPLE OF THE WORLD, UNITE!
YOU HAVE NOTHING TO LOSE....

Originally published by the Fat Underground, Los Angeles, California, USA.

A big fat thank you to...

Thank you to the Yard, the Roundhouse, Nuffield Theatres Southampton and Arts Council England for their support in making the show. Thank you to Storytelling PR for keeping us sane in Edinburgh, and the Mann Bros for their film work. Thank you to our additional Stage Managers, Jasmine Davies and Frances Allison. And to Mr Hallen whose kindness and wisdom is at the heart of everything I make.

To the whole FFF team who have been incredibly generous with their creativity, spirit and rehearsal room snacks. Thank you especially to Dais for knowing how to bring the show to life, even when I didn't.

To my wonderful friends, about whom I could fill a whole book with the reasons why I love and am grateful for. I hope one day I can pay you back for all the laughter, dancing, tickets bought, tears dried, helium balloons rescued, rambling voice notes and secrets kept. There is simply no way I could ever have got here without you.

To my family whose support, generosity and love has never waived. Thank you for everything you've done to help lay the foundations for the person I've become.

And finally thank you to fat activists and artists that have fought (and continue to) so tirelessly and selflessly so work like mine can exist. I am forever indebted to you.